SEATTLE

THE GROWTH OF THE CITY

SEATTLE
THE GROWTH OF THE CITY

Alexander Holmes

CHARTWELL
BOOKS, INC.

This edition published in 2007 by

CHARTWELL BOOKS, INC.
A Division of
BOOK SALES, INC.
114 Northfield Avenue
Edison, New Jersey 08837

ISBN-13: 978-0-7858-2210-3
ISBN-10: 0-7858-2210-0

© 2007 Compendium Publishing, 43 Frith Street, London,
Soho, W1V 4SA, United Kingdom

Cataloging-in-Publication data is available from the Library
of Congress

Printed and bound in China

Design: Ian Hughes/Compendium Design

Page 2: Named for the band of Seattle native Jimi Hendrix, The Experience
Music Project was designed by architect Frank Gehry and inspired by a
broken Fender Stratocaster guitar.
Page 4: The classic view over downtown Seattle from Queen Anne.

Contents

Introduction

Drawn from a similar point of view as the map on pages six and seven, this panorama shows how the city has grown just five years later in 1884. Note how deforestation now extends all the way to Lake Union and Lake Washington, while the city itself is more densely built and larger industrial and commercial buildings are beginning to appear.

The party began to establish their town of small wooden cabins, while a more recent arrival, David S. "Doc" Maynard, set up Seattle's first store at present-day South Main Street and First Avenue South. By 1852, King County had been created and Seattle named as county seat. With the arrival in 1853 of Henry Yesler, the fledgling city welcomed its first industrialist. In return for land, Yesler constructed a steam-powered lumber mill and Seattle was suddenly in business. Trees from the forests surrounding the city were slid down Mill Street (later known as Skid Road, today's Yesler Way), processed at the mill, and shipped off, mainly to boom town San Francisco, which was expanding rapidly as the hub of the Californian Gold Rush.

Despite the early Seattleites wrangling over land claims (a problem that still has repercussions in the confusing layout of Yesler Way), the small town grew quickly. Just three years after the original settlement, Seattle had a population of 300, a roaring trade in lumber, and a hotel that also served as a restaurant and brothel ruled over by Mary Conklin. Unfortunately, the town was about to experience its first reversal of fortune. In January of 1855 the Point Elliott Treaty was signed, awarding almost all Native-American lands in western Washington to the United States. The tribes who had been so

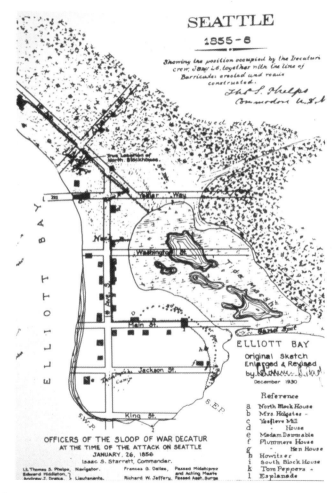

RIGHT: This map, copied from the original in 1930, is a rare view of the settlement just four years after its founding. Note the handful of buildings clustered along the waterfront. Marked "e" in the south-west corner of town is "Madam Damnable," the name by which sharp-tongued Irishwoman Mary Conklin was better known. Her establishment was the town's hotel, restaurant, and bordello. Among the other places noted are Yesler's mill and the blockhouse where settlers took refuge from Native-American forces. The map describes "Hills and Woods thronged with Indians."

This map, entitled "Bird's-Eye View of the City of Seattle," is a detailed depiction of the small metropolis in 1878. On the large dock with ships at port are the Yesler lumber mill buildings on which the city's initial prosperity depended. Timber would have been slid down Mill Street to the mill, sawn, and loaded on to ships. In the foreground are steamships, which began to ply the route between Seattle and San Francisco in 1875. At this time Seattle's population would have been around 3,000 and almost the entire town was made from wood.

Introduction

Perched on the rainy northwestern edge of the United States, Seattle has evolved from a tiny settlement of a few log cabins to an incredibly diverse and dynamic city that has made a global impact in just sixteen decades. Today, the largest metropolis in Washington State and the hub of the Pacific Northwest's commerce, it is also one of the United States' most beautiful cities. Almost completely surrounded by the waters of Puget Sound, lakes Washington and

BELOW: This photograph, taken after the Great Seattle Fire of June 6, 1889, illustrates the devastation wreaked by the flames. Few of downtown's buildings have been left standing, and those are damaged beyond repair. The fire began in the basement of a shop on First Avenue and Madison Street when a young apprentice spilled boiling glue over wood shavings.

His accident eventually proved a blessing for the city. As rebuilding work got underway, engineers raised the level of the streets to eradicate Seattle's drainage problem. Many of the buildings constructed in the fire's aftermath remain and are superb examples of Victorian architecture.

Union, and numerous rivers, its downtown skyscrapers look out on a landscape of pine-forested hills with views of the Cascade and Olympic mountain ranges.

Seattle's relative youth belies a rich history and one that its citizens have fought hard to preserve and build upon. With a metropolitan population approaching 600,000, a lively arts, music, and cultural scene, which has spawned famous "grunge" rock bands, and a slightly quirky personality that is completely different to that of any other American city, Seattle is a dynamic and charming place with much to boast about. Not bad for a city that was only founded in the mid-nineteenth century.

While the area was inhabited for thousands of years by the Suquamish and Duwamish tribes, the story of Seattle's growth as a city begins with the arrival of a handful of settlers at West Seattle's Alki Beach on November 13, 1851. Headed by Arthur A. Denny, the party of twenty-four men, women, and children set up camp, naming their settlement New York Alki, the latter word translating from Chinook as "by and by." Their choice of name gives a sense of the pioneers' ambition for their new town. In order to achieve their grand plans, the settlers were persuaded to relocate the following spring.

Taking the advice of the friendly chief of the local tribes and finding that Elliott Bay would provide a superior harbor for the city they imagined, almost all of the Denny party moved to the site of present day Pioneer Square, and this time christened their town for the chief who had so helpfully steered them—Seattle.

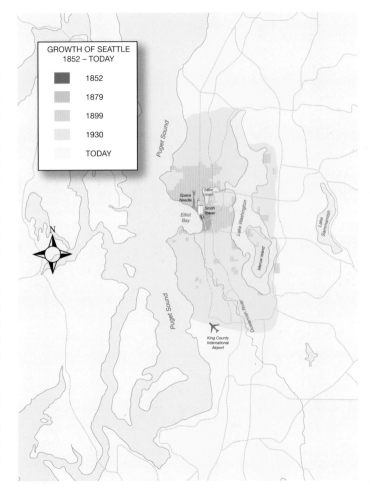

MOUNT RAINIER
14,440 FT.

LAKE UNION

LAKE WASHI

OLYMPIC RANGE 6 TO 10,000 FT. HIGH.

RIGHT: This panorama shows how the city has changed and grown by 1891. Following the Great Fire of 1889, and due to the city's success, all the buildings around downtown are now imposing brick structures while many more docks and businesses cling to the waterfront. The railroad has also arrived. In fact, the first transcontinental train reached Seattle just the year before this map was drawn, though Seattle's first service, carrying coal, began in 1872.

BELOW: Early Seattle was surrounded by seven hills. Following the fire it was decided that Denny Hill was an obstruction to commercial traffic and in a massive feat of engineering much of it was washed away between 1899 and 1912. Thousands of millions of gallons of water were pumped from Lake Union and sprayed under high pressure on the hill. The resulting liquefied clay and rocks were sluiced away.

RIGHT: A view over Seattle and Puget Sound at the end of the nineteenth century.

helpful to Seattle's first residents were to be relocated. Understandably resentful of such treatment, a war party of local tribes attacked Seattle in January of 1856. The Battle of Seattle lasted only a day and ended with the rout of the Native-Americans at the hands of settlers aided by marines and the guns of U.S.S. *Decatur* for the loss of only two of the townsfolk. Ill feeling would, however, continue to seethe for years to come.

Nevertheless, Seattle was soon back to work and the following years saw it grow apace. By 1860, the town was connected by road to other Washington settlements and the following year proudly opened Washington Territorial University, thus founding the University of Washington. In 1863, news was disseminated through the city's first newspaper, *The Gazette*. By the end of the decade Seattle also had its first public library and now boasted a population of over a thousand. They would be joined throughout the 1870s by many more settlers, notably hundreds of Chinese who were brought in to work on the rail line that joined Seattle to Newcastle in 1872 and in King County's newly opened coal mines. Other developments of the 1870s included the construction of Seattle's first brick building, its first hospital, the start of a regular steamship service to San Francisco, and the opening of the city's first theater, Squire's Opera House on First Avenue South. The city's population had more than tripled in just ten years.

The 1880s bought Seattle further developments, such as the start of the horse-drawn trolley service, as well as a massive influx of new citizens. However, the decade was a difficult one for the city. Economic stress caused many Seattleites of European extraction to resent the growing Chinese community. Rioting in 1886 was followed by the expulsion of several hundred Chinese. Then, in 1889, the city suffered its worst setback so far. A basement fire that started in a store on First Avenue ravaged the wooden buildings and boardwalks of the city, destroying thirty blocks within a day. Much of the downtown area was razed.

The fire offered the city the chance of a new beginning. With its thrown together wooden buildings gone, downtown was regraded, bringing street level much higher and eradicating the problem of Seattle's perpetually muddy roads. Well-designed brick buildings sprang up, often on top of older structures. Today, it is possible to explore the original buildings beneath the old on the Underground Tour that operates from Doc Maynard's Public House.

As the nineteenth century drew to a close Seattle was to experience its greatest surge of growth yet. In 1897, the ship *Portland* famously docked in Seattle with a cargo of gold from northern Yukon, sparking the great Klondike Gold Rush. Seattle was perfectly positioned as a jumping off point for prospectors on their way to make their fortunes and its merchants and bankers were equally well placed to exploit gold fever. All miners were legally obliged to equip themselves with a years worth of provisions and Seattle's tradesfolk happily outfitted them, in many cases reaping much bigger profits than the prospectors. The city's bankers also benefited from the huge influx of gold, while new bars, brothels, and theaters catered to successful prospectors celebrating their new fortunes. Tens of thousands of people on

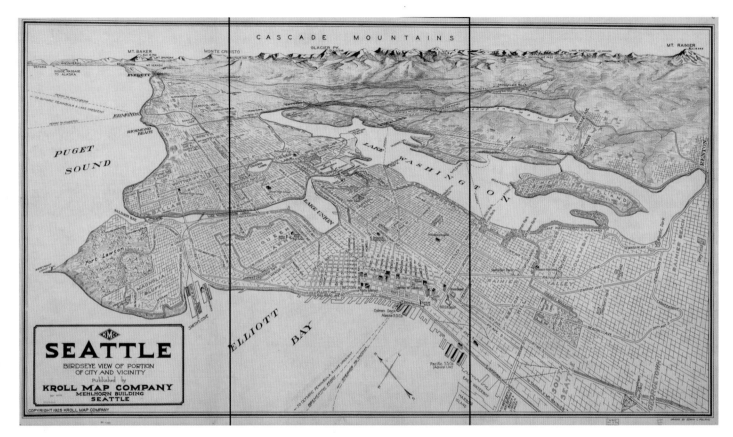

ABOVE: Drawn in 1925, this bird's-eye map shows how the city has again swollen since 1891; where before there were sporadic buildings outside the cluster of Pioneer Square, residential Seattle now stretches far to the north, east, and south. A swathe of annexations had added many neighborhoods to the city in the early twentieth century. Also apparent is Fort Lawton, built on Magnolia Bluff in 1900, and the new Lake Washington Canal, completed in 1917. The few buildings that are noted by name include 1914's Smith Tower and Pioneer Square's totem pole.

17

their way to the gold fields passed through the city within a few short years and a percentage elected to stay. As the twentieth century opened the city that was not even fifty years old had a population of over 80,000, a department store (Frederick & Nelson), another new seat of learning in Seattle College, and had recently bought an estate with its own menagerie from Guy Phinney. Woodland Park Zoo was born.

Seattle's rapid expansion continued well into the new century and with the development of steel-frame construction techniques growth began to reach upward as well as marching out into what had previously been suburbs. When Smith Tower opened in 1914 it became the tallest building west of the Mississippi, a title it would hold until 1962. It presided over a city that was by now recognized as the heart of the Pacific Northwest and was bigger than ever. Ballard, West Seattle, Columbia City, and Rainier Beach had become annexed to the city in 1907, followed by Laurelhurst and Georgetown in 1909. Downtown was now expanding along Second and Third avenues, leaving Pioneer Square behind. In 1909, the city also hosted a World's Fair, the spectacular Alaska-Yukon-Pacific Exposition. Its population by now was approaching quarter of a million.

The advent of World War I saw a jump in orders for Seattle's lumber, while new shipyards opened along the coast. However it was in 1916, when William Boeing constructed his first aircraft in Seattle, that the city had its first taste of future prosperity. By the time that World War II started Boeing was firmly established as an aircraft manufacturer and the planes his factories made, including the B-17 and B-29 bombers, led air assaults in all theaters of combat. As production increased, the city reaped the benefits and when hostilities ceased Boeing turned to civilian transport aircraft, pioneering a new age of travel and giving jobs for tens of thousands as well as wealth for the city. While its headquarters moved to Chicago in 2001, the company is still one of Seattle's biggest employers.

Between the wars Seattle had continued its seemingly inexhaustible growth, building Lake Washington Ship Canal, Aurora Bridge, and Lake Washington Floating Bridge, as well as completing a regrade of Denny Hill, and opening parks and the Seattle Art Museum. Along the way, Seattle had become the first United States city to elect a female mayor, Bertha Landes, who took office 1926. Like the rest of America, Seattle suffered during the Great Depression, not least historic Pioneer Square, which as "Skid Row" entered the American lexicon. The once stately Victorian buildings became seedy hotels and the square slipped into a decline from which it would not recover for decades. However, a return to prosperity at the end of the thirties saw the city growing once more as ever more people came in search of a better life, swelling the neighborhoods further from downtown. In 1953, the city's limits moved again, this time as far as North 145th

LEFT: Seattle in January 1962 showing the Monorail and Space Needle newly constructed for the World's Fair (building had been completed in the previous month). Behind the 605-foot Space Needle downtown's spectacular skyline is yet to rise above the 467-foot standard set by Smith Tower in 1914.

Street and in the same year the Alaskan Way Viaduct was completed, replacing outdated rail tracks and helping motor vehicles to access the city center. In 1962, Seattle hosted its second World's Fair, which bequeathed the city Seattle Center, the Monorail, and in the Space Needle one of the world's most recognizable buildings. The city also began to take stock of its architectural heritage at the end of the sixties, making Pioneer Square it first historic district and paving the way for the restoration of the area's buildings and its reputation.

Throughout the remainder of the twentieth century and into the new millennium Seattle has become firmly established on the world stage. The little settlement with its single lumber mill now occupies nearly 150 square miles and has added a number of architecturally noted skyscrapers to its distinctive skyline. Renowned for cutting edge technology, a liberal ethos that fosters the arts, and the sophistication of its inhabitants, the Emerald City is well on the way to fulfilling the ambitions of its founders. If Seattle's rate of growth is maintained, given another century and a half it will indeed rival New York.

LEFT: Today's Seattle downtown skyline. The black tower behind and to the right of the photograph is Seattle's tallest building, the 882.5-foot Columbia Center. To the left of Columbia Center, Smith Tower provides scale. To the right, the second highest building is Washington Mutual Tower (772 feet). The third highest building in the city, to the right again, is the 740-foot Two Union Square.

First Steps: 1851-1879

This aerial photograph shows Alki Point where the Denny Party, Seattle's original white settlers arrived and spent their first winter, which was—in typical Seattle fashion—extremely wet. The settlement was named New York Alki, the "alki" being a Chinook word that translates as "[by and]"

First Steps: 1851-1879

From the moment that they set foot on Alki Beach in the cold November of 1851, the original members of the Denny Party nurtured grand ambitions for their new lands. Having spent months of hardship crossing the continent, these hardy and determined souls were intent on establishing a successful community that would grow to rival New York itself. Fortunately for them, the hundreds and then thousands of people who followed them to this then remote bay on the northwest Pacific coast shared their ambitions. Having moved to the shore of Elliott Bay during the early spring after their arrival, Arthur A. Denny, his brother David, and their small group of pioneers were soon joined by enterprising souls such as Henry Yesler, a lumberman who was tempted to build a sawmill in Seattle by offers of land, Charles Plummer, and David "Doc" Maynard. Yesler's mill, the natural harbor of Elliott Bay, the abundant forests around those first log cabin homes, and the wealth of San Francisco down the coast combined to give Seattle the initial impetus it needed.

When King County was founded in 1852, Maynard, who had political connections, saw to it that Seattle was named as the county seat. Within a few short years what had been a tiny settlement clustered around the site of present day Pioneer Square had a thriving lumber business, stores, a restaurant/hotel/bordello, a school, a hospital, and churches. As trade increased and the

By 1875, Seattle was beginning to look like a frontier town rather than a small settlement. This photograph taken along First Avenue toward Yesler's steam-powered mill, shows townspeople gathered in front of Seattle's stores, including the Pioneer Drug Store.

population grew, one thing that Seattle lacked was women, a shortfall which Asa Mercer corrected in 1864 by traveling to the East Coast and bringing back with him fifty-seven young women to become wives for the settlers and help civilize Seattle. While hardly challenging New York, by 1879 Seattle was a firmly established town with a population of around 3,500, its own newspaper, a burgeoning coal mining industry, its first brick buildings, a rail connection to western Washington, and even an Opera House—Squire's on First Avenue South. Though its streets were still waterlogged and boarded over, Seattle had made an impressive start.

LEFT: This embroidered sampler, dating to 1853, depicts the first Seattle home of Arthur A. Denny at Marion Street and First Avenue. Denny was the leader of the small party of settlers who set out along the Oregon Trail in 1851 and eventually reached Alki Point, staking claims there before moving across Elliott Bay in the early spring of 1852. The new site of Seattle was selected under advice from Duwamish chief Sealth, for whom the settlement was later named.

RIGHT: One of Seattle's earliest new arrivals, in 1853, was Charles Plummer. Although too late to claim any of the best land, he opened the successful store (pictured) and then bought a sawmill and a coalmine. The entrepreneurial Plummer later used his profits to start a waterworks, a brickyard, a livery stable, and also bought the hotel previously run by "Mother Damnable" Mary Conklin, naming it Conklin House after her.

LEFT: Central to the rapid growth of the settlement, the mill also supplied sawdust with which the bay's mudflats were filled and boards that were laid on top. Nevertheless, until the Great Fire of 1889 Seattle was perpetually wallowing in mud.

As time progressed and orders flowed in for his timber, Yesler was able to build a wharf where timber had been previously rafted out to waiting vessels. This undated photograph would have been taken around 1870.

ABOVE: Providence Hospital, Seattle's first proper medical facility, opened its doors at Fifth and Madison on August 2, 1878. The hospital was designed by Mother Joseph, who taught herself architecture for that purpose and built under her watchful eye. It was run by the Sisters of Charity of Providence. This photograph shows the hospital in the early twentieth century, soon after additional building work created the blocks on each wing of the structure.

A view north along the Seattle waterfront from Yesler's wharf in 1878. The mill has already deforested much of the surrounding area and Seattle's citizens, who now number around 3,000, are beginning to build their homes further away from the Pioneer Square area. The columned white building on the horizon toward the center of the panorama is Washington Territorial University, which opened on May 21, 1861 with thirty pupils of all ages and one teacher. The University moved to a new site in 1895, stopped teaching the younger students, and eventually became the University of Washington.

356 X

LEFT AND ABOVE: Founded in the early 1878 by Edward Sweeney, Rainier Beer became one of the United States' largest breweries after a series of mergers that began a decade later with the acquisition of two other companies. These photographs show the first Rainier Brewery, located in Georgetown, in 1886 and the plant that was built on the same site when Prohibition ended. The company's large red "R" was later enlarged and lit up in neon and became a Seattle landmark.

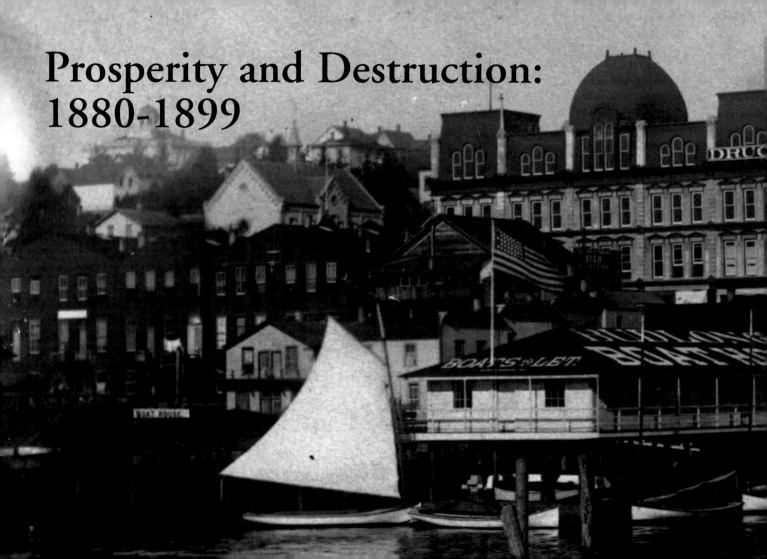

Prosperity and Destruction: 1880-1899

This photograph of the Seattle waterfront, taken shortly before the fire, shows Budlong's Boathouse and the YMCA (founded in 1876) as well as other Seattle landmarks. Despite an economically turbulent decade, which saw the expulsion of hundreds of Chinese citizens in 1886, Seattle is growing quickly.

Prosperity and Destruction: 1880-1899

The 1800s bought difficult times to Seattle. Its dreams of great prosperity were shared with other close-by towns—Tacoma, Bellingham, and Port Townsend—and each vied to become the terminus on the new Northern Pacific Railroad, which would connect Puget Sound to the East and boost trade opportunities. Unfortunately, Seattle lost out to Tacoma in 1883, and had to be content with having seen the first trans-Pacific steamship off from Elliott Bay, itself a significant point in the city's development as a major port. The decade also bought a downturn in the city's economic fortunes, which led to ugly scenes with Seattle's Chinese population who were believed to be taking jobs that rightfully belonged to white Americans. The troubles culminatied in the Anti-Chinese Riots of 1886 and the forced expulsion of hundreds of Seattle's new citizens. At the end of the decade, a fire that had started in a store basement blazed through the mostly wooden city, totally destroying downtown.

Nevertheless, Seattle dusted itself down and looked once more to the future. Rebuilding work began, this time in brick and on regraded land that eliminated the perennial drainage problem of Seattle's streets. Most of the buildings in the Pioneer Square district date from this period. Buoyed by the successful engineering work downtown, Seattle also began razing Denny Hill, which for so long had obstructed horse-drawn traffic. The jets of water that would eventually wear the hill away started up in 1899, by which time Seattle was in the midst of another boom. The city was the perfect jumping off point for gold prospectors headed north to the newly discovered gold mines of the Yukon and fortunes were made from outfitting and entertaining miners. With a population of over 80,000 by the end of the century, Seattle was bigger than ever. Where the slopes of Queen Anne and First Hill had been sparsely populated, they became thickly covered with ever grander homes, while streetcars allowed workers to travel to neighborhoods further from downtown than ever before.

RIGHT: As the new decade, dawned Seattle was still a city of mud and boardwalks. This photograph from 1880 shows father and son, identified as A.W. and Walter Piper walking their dog, Jim, along Front Street.

Front St. Seattle W.T.

Downtown in 1882 was an area of smallholdings with Yesler's mill and wharfs the only structures of note along Elliott Bay. The following two decades would see the area transformed into a small but thriving city.

Although Seattle's most prosperous years were still to come, this Independence Day parade up First Avenue in the early 1880s gives an excellent impression of how Seattle had grown in the years before the fire. There are many more stores housed in larger, more imposing buildings. While many are still of wood, brick structures are beginning to appear.

A view over Seattle from atop Denny Hill in 1884. The city is unmistakably thriving. Commercial buildings are concentrated along the waterfont and homes now stretch further back from the shore. Puget Sound is thick with ships arriving to take on shipments of lumber.

LEFT: Although settlement of Queen Anne Hill began soon after the Denny Party arrived, it was not until the early to mid-1880s that it earned its name, which was bestowed upon it due to the numerous Queen Anne-style houses that Seattle's business elite built upon its slopes. Today, the area retains many of its original buildings and it is still one of the city's most well-to-do neighborhoods.

RIGHT: In 1887, lumber tycoon Guy C. Phinney purchased land for his Woodland Park estate. The grounds—landscaped into beautiful formal gardens complete with promenades, a conservatory, and a menagerie—were generously opened to the public (though strict rules of conduct were imposed). Phinney died in 1893 and Seattle purchased the estate for $100,000 in 1899, thus founding Woodland Park Zoo.

ABOVE AND RIGHT: Seattle's first horse-drawn streetcar took to the streets on September 23, 1884. Instantly popular with Seattleites, it was soon joined by the cars of other companies offering different routes and services—the first cable cars started in 1887 and electrified routes were in operation by 1889. These early public transport networks helped move residents out to the growing suburbs and were so popular that by the middle of the next decade no less than twenty-two different companies were running services. All of these were brought under the umbrella of the Seattle Electric Railway Company in 1898. Unfortunately, these fine old streetcars were outdated by the beginning of the 1940s and all routes were closed down, though the Waterfront Streetcar began a new service in 1982.

LEFT: Built in 1883 at James Street and Yesler Way to replace an earlier hotel dating to 1861, the Occidental Hotel, at the center of this photograph, also housed the Puget Sound National Bank on its ground floor.

ABOVE: This photo graphically illustrates the extent to which Seattle was ravaged by the Great Fire of June 6, 1889. The picture shows almost exactly the same view as that on the opposite page.

LEFT: The replacement hotel, now renamed Hotel Seattle, occupied the same site as its predecessor and was architecturally similar. The hotel was demolished in 1961 to make way for a parking garage, an act of vandalism that sparked debate about Seattle's historic buildings and culminated in Pioneer Square being designated a historic district.

RIGHT: With two Seattleites giving a sense of scale, this photograph was taken along Front Street on June 7, 1889, the day after the fire. Smoking ruins are all that remains of the bustling waterfront thoroughfare.

Deprived of their premises by the fire, many Seattle businesses continued to operate from makeshift huts and tents. This photograph, taken along Second Avenue and Marion Street is dated July 1889.

In the aftermath of the fire, Seattle wasted no time in rebuilding. Just over a year later, in July of 1890, downtown is already beginning to take on its new appearance.

LEFT: Beneath Pioneer Square are the remains of buildings that were once at ground level. When the area was regraded after the fire, many new structures were erected on top of the remains of the old, which were then forgotten about. Rediscovered in the late sixties, it is now possible to tour underground Seattle. The most popular starting point is Doc Maynard's pub on Pioneer Square.

RIGHT: Designed by Elmer Fisher in the wake of the fire, the Austin A. Bell apartment building in downtown is an impressive work of architecture that incorporates elements of Richardson Romanesque, Gothic, and Italianate styles. Unfortunately, Austin A. Bell did not live to see the building he commissioned completed as the troubled Seattleite committed suicide soon after approving the plans.

BELOW AND RIGHT: Jutting out into Lake Union, Seattle's Eastlake neighborhood became an increasingly popular residential area when electric trams reached north of downtown in 1890. In 1891 it was incorporated into the city and grand houses began to spring up. Eastlake's gasworks, built in 1906 can be seen by the shore of the black and white photograph. Considered an environmental hazard as well as an eyesore by the time the plant closed in 1956, the site was redesignated in 1975 and became Gas Works Park.

LEFT: Typical of the new architecture that arose in downtown Seattle, and also designed by Elmer Fisher, is the Pioneer Building. Occupying the site of Henry Yesler's first mill, the terra cotta and red brick office building was completed in 1892.

RIGHT: 1897 saw the arrival of the ship *Portland* in Seattle Harbor, loaded with two tons of gold from the Yukon. The discovery sparked the legendary Klondike Gold Rush and also bolstered Seattle's fortunes. Over 40,000 prospectors passed through the city on the way to Alaska and many citizens grew wealthy from outfitting them at stores such as these.

LEFT AND RIGHT: There has been a totem pole in Pioneer Square since October 18, 1899, when the first was erected to cheers from the crowd, a gift from fifteen members of the Chamber of Commerce recently returned from a tour of Alaska. Unfortunately, it soon came to light that the pole had been stolen from a Tlingit village during their travels. The thieving pillars of the community countered that the village was deserted, but it was found that most of the residents had just been away fishing at the time. Eight of the men were later indicted by an Alaskan grand jury. The case was finally settled amicably with a payment of $500 to the Tlingits, who later carved a replica of the pole when the first was damaged by fire in 1940. The replacement stands in the same spot today.

Washington University

Officially opened in 1861 at its original address in downtown Seattle and then known as Washington Territorial University, the seat of learning had a shaky beginning, coming close to being closed down for lack of funds and lack of students. However, by 1895 it had outgrown its first building and moved to its present site northeast of downtown on Lake Washington. Development of the area was slow at first (1895's Denny Hall was the first building on campus), but the university was aided by the 1909 Alaska-Yukon-Pacific Exposition, which was built on the campus grounds and left behind it buildings, such as Architecture Hall and Cunningham Hall, that the university could utilize. Since then the University of Washington or "U Dub" as it is locally known, has almost continually added new facilities to the campus, including many fine works of architecture.

RIGHT AND FAR RIGHT: The exterior and graduate reading room of Washington University's famous Suzzallo Library, which was built in a Gothic style in 1916 having outgrown its original quarters in a building designed for the 1909 exposition.

LEFT: Built in 1920 and expanded over the years to seat 72,500, Husky Stadium is home to Washington University's Huskies football team and one of the most scenic stadiums in the country.

RIGHT: The Drumheller Fountain, in Frosh Pond, was built to celebrate the university's centennial in 1961. The pond itself dates back to the 1909 exposition and is traditionally used for dunking freshmen.

An aerial view of the University of Washington 639-acre campus. Today's university is the largest in the Northwest—35,000 students are taught and housed in over 200 buildings.

The New Century: 1900-1913

The 1909 Alaska-Yukon-Pacific Exposition was a major landmark in the city's growth. Attracting an average of nearly 80,000 visitors a day over that summer, the fair firmly established Seattle as the capital of the Northwest and left behind many of Washington University's major buildings. Among the more bizarre exhibits were a life-size elephant made of nuts, a thirty foot pyramid of pineapples, and clams—not sculpted into any shape, just clams as nature intended. A more exciting exhibit was a million dollars worth of Yukon gold. This panoramic photograph shows the Arctic Circle buildings that were the hub of the exposition.

The New Century: 1900-1913

The Klondike Gold Rush was to give Seattle its most prosperous years yet and many arrived in the city to share in the wealth being generated. Not only did the Seattle's population top 100,000 for the first time, but by the end of the first decade of the twentieth century it had jumped to a staggering 237,194. As the neighborhoods spread ever outward—reached now by electric streetcars and the motor cars that were being manufactured at Seattle Car Manufacturing—Ballard, West Seattle, Columbia City, and Rainier Beach were annexed in 1907, to be followed by Laurelhurst and Georgetown in 1910. Gold was not the only source of wealth though; as well as controlling most of the shipping to Alaska, Seattle was trading further overseas with other nations around the Pacific Rim. Along with the returning Chinese, Japanese immigrants now swelled the city's population and from the east, Scandinavians arrived, headed for the industrial sawmills that would have dwarfed Henry Yesler's original mill. Seattle was now also firmly attached to the rest of the nation by rail. The Great Northern and Pacific and Northern Pacific railroads rolled into the new King Street Station in 1906, while in 1911, Union Station opened, welcoming trains of the Union Pacific.

These heady days saw new buildings rising in downtown, which now started breaking away from Pioneer Square. The Alaska Building was the first skyscraper to grace the city's skyline, while on the ground Seattle also began to bloom thanks to the Olmsted brothers, who were commissioned in 1903 to create the network of parks that help make Seattle such a beautiful city to this day.

While Seattle's fame was already spreading, the Alaska-Yukon-Pacific Exposition of 1909 sealed its reputation as the pre-eminent city of the Northwest Pacific. Celebrating the ten year anniversary of the arrival of the first cargo of gold onboard the *Portland* (the exposition was delayed by two years), this World's Fair was an enormous success, bringing exhibits from the Pacific Rim ports that Seattle now reached as well as hundreds of thousands of visitors.

RIGHT: Volunteer Park has been a part of the Seattle cityscape since forty acres were purchased for $2,000 in 1876. Designated a cemetery in 1885, it became a public park in 1887 and landscaping began. Renamed Volunteer Park in 1901, the task was completed in 1904 by the Olmsted brothers, the sons of Frederick Law Olmsted, designer of New York's Central Park. The Olmsteds were hired in 1903 to create Seattle's park system and over the next thirty-three years they designed the network of superb parks and recreational facilities that Seattleites enjoy to this day.

LEFT AND RIGHT: 1904's Alaska Building on Cherry Street and Second Avenue was the first steel-framed skyscraper in the city, and also the tallest until the 1911 Hoge Building was completed. Designed by Earmes & Young it rises fourteen stories to 182-feet-high and is distinctively decorated with walrus heads.

Seattle has had a public library since 1869, but it was not until this building opened in 1906 that its books found a permanent home. Former libraries included the Occidental Building, Rialto Building, and Yesler Mansion. The latter was destroyed by fire in 1901 and every book—apart from those on loan—was lost. The replacement library was funded with a donation of $220,000 from philanthropist Andrew Carnegie.

ABOVE: Listed on the National Register of Historic Places, Pike Place Market is one of Seattle's best-loved landmarks. The market traces its roots back to August 1907, when a handful of farmers pulled their carts into Pike Place and began to sell their produce directly to the crowds, cutting out local "commission houses" that had been making large and unfair profits. A huge success with Seattleites from that first morning, the first market building was set up to protect the wagons by the end of November. Over the years the market buildings expanded and now cover nine acres.

Dedicated just a few days before Christmas in 1907, St. James' Cathedral on First Hill is one of Seattle's most impressive works of architecture. With its distinctive twin 167-foot towers, architects Heins and LaFarge designed the cathedral in an Italian Renaissance style.

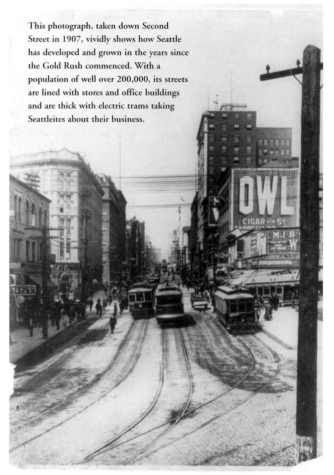

This photograph, taken down Second Street in 1907, vividly shows how Seattle has developed and grown in the years since the Gold Rush commenced. With a population of well over 200,000, its streets are lined with stores and office buildings and are thick with electric trams taking Seattleites about their business.

1907 also saw a gas station open at Holgate Street and Western Avenue. Built by John McLean and operated by Standard Oil, it was the first of its kind in the nation.

Seattle's growing wealth and population saw its neighborhoods become increasingly built-up during the first decade of the twentieth century. First Hill, seen here in 1911, was one of the most elegantly exclusive and boasted some of the city's first upscale apartment buildings.

The Denny Regrade

To the north of downtown area is an area known as the Denny Regrade, which includes the Belltown neighborhood, once the site of a large hill that was too steep to be climbed by horse-drawn traffic and which obstructed Seattle's expansion to the north. To overcome this problem a massive engineering feat was proposed by city engineer Reginald Heber Thomson. Denny Hill was to be literally washed away. The plans were confounded for some years, however, by Arthur Denny himself. The Seattle founder tried and failed to make the hill the seat of state government, then set about building the elaborate Denny Hotel on its crest (later finished by James A. Moore and renamed the Washington Hotel). When Moore was financially forced to move to premises closer to downtown in 1906, Thomson was finally able to begin work on the removal of Denny Hill. Although the final phase of the regrade was not complete until the 1930s, over the next five years high-powered jets of water pumped from Lake Union were played on the hill and the rocks and earth sluiced into Elliott Bay.

RIGHT: This 1907 photograph shows the Washington Hotel as Denny Hill is sluiced away around it.

LEFT: Any property owners who refused to sell found their homes left stranded in the air as the hill was carved away around them. The resulting towers of earth and rock topped with abandoned homes were nicknamed "spite mounds" and eventually collapsed.

RIGHT: During the final decades of the twentieth century the Denny Regrade area was transformed. Nightclubs, galleries, cafés, and trendy stores such as Belltown's Jet City antique shop completely changed the area's character.

Unfortunately, for many years the intended commercial success of the area never materialized and it became a cheap rent district of apartment buildings, warehouses, and car lots until late in the twentieth century when it began to attract Seattle's Bohemian artists and musicians. This photograph, taken in 1978, shows the area on the cusp of a mini boom.

LEFT: Pioneer Place's ornate pergola was erected in 1909 over luxurious public restrooms and became a national historic landmark (along with the square's totem pole) in 1977.

RIGHT: The First United Methodist Church on Fifth Avenue and Marion Street is a direct descendant of the first church in Seattle, the First Methodist Episcopal, which was built in 1855. This building, which dates to 1910 is the third church to house the congregation.

LEFT: 1911 saw the opening of Union Station (originally Oregon and Washington Station) at Fourth Avenue South and South Jackson Street. The terminus provided a service to Chicago, which connected Seattle to the East Coast.

RIGHT AND OVERLEAF: Seattle had been a busy port since the first timber was slid down to Yesler's Mill, and by the turn of the century the waterfront was a jumble of businesses, wharves, and warehouses as can be seen in this black and white photograph, which dates to 1904. In 1912, the city responded by creating the Port of Seattle to manage waterfront development. Since then Seattle has become one of the world's leading ports, creating thousands of jobs for the city and bringing in billions of dollars in revenue.

Purchased in 1912 and erected by park staff, the Volunteer Park Conservatory houses rare and exotic plants from around the globe. It now encompasses five buildings, which house collections of bromeliads, palms, ferns, cacti, and seasonal displays.

War and Peace: 1914–1945

The waterfront in 1917 is a good indication for the city's success as a port. Where once Yesler's wharf was the sole dock, now piers and warehouses line Elliott Bay.

War and Peace: 1914–1945

Unlike so many other cities around the world, the two world wars bought even more prosperity to Seattle. During the first conflict the city enjoyed a massively increased demand for its lumber, while workers found ready employment at the shipyards along Puget Sound. At the same time the newly opened Panama Canal boosted trade with ports around the Pacific that were untouched by the war. Most importantly, in 1916 an aviator by the name of William Boeing designed his first aircraft, a pontoon biplane, and went on to build a manufacturing plant, and in 1928 an airfield. During World War II, Boeing was of vital importance to the American war effort, producing the B-17 and B-29 bombers that did so much to help win the war. For Boeing this meant massive

defense contracts, and Seattle reaped the benefits as the wealth spread out into the city.

Between the wars, Seattle grew steadily larger, though the pace of expansion had slowed somewhat from its Gold Rush peak. By 1920 the population topped 300,000, who could now choose to live in tall new apartment buildings while working in the city's steadily growing number of skyscrapers, presided over by 1914's Smith Tower. City officials were also making steady improvements to the city's infrastructure, building bridges to aid the flow of traffic around the ever larger city and completing the final phase of the Denny Hill regrade. Sophisticated Seattleites could also now enjoy the artworks on exhibit at the Seattle Art Museum, which opened in Volunteer Park in 1933 and afterward join the whirl at the Olympic Hotel, the luxurious center of the Seattle Social scene since 1926.

BELOW: An old Seattle landmark that opened its doors in 1914 was Dugdale Athletics Park in Rainier Valley, the first double-decker stadium on the West Coast. Tragically burned to the ground by an arsonist on July 4, 1939, the park was home to the Seattle Indians.

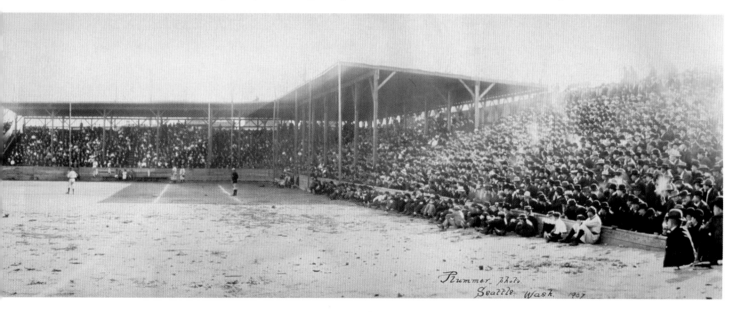

Smith Tower

L.C. Smith
42 Story
Building

Under construction ~ Seattle

Lyman Cornelius Smith arrived in Seattle from New York in 1909. During his years in the Big Apple he had witnessed the rise of the city's first skyscrapers as well as the publicity they were generating for the companies that built them. Smith was determined to follow suit. Originally planning a much less ambitious building to house his typewriter company, he was persuaded by his son to set his sights ever higher. The result was the steel-framed L.C. Smith Tower, completed in 1914. Holding the title of tallest building west of the Mississippi for nearly fifty years, the elegant 465-foot building provided Smith with as much media attention as he could have wished for and remains a much-loved Seattle landmark to this day.

LEFT: Smith Tower nearing completion in 1913. The architectural firm hired by Smith was Gaggin & Gaggin of Syracuse, whose tallest building to date was a mere five stories and who would never attempt another project of this size again.

RIGHT: Photographed soon after its completion in 1914, Smith Tower is obviously influenced by New York's Woolworth Building, though it has less of its inspiration's ornate decoration. Nevertheless, its simplicity lends it a clean and light appearance.

FAR RIGHT: Nearly a century after it first opened it doors, and now overshadowed by the Columbia Center to the right of the photograph, the Smith Tower is an integral part of the Seattle skyline and one of the world's most instantly recognizable buildings.

BELOW AND RIGHT: Looking toward Elliott Bay across the railroad yards from Beacon Hill in 1914. The clock tower in the center of the photograph marks the King Street Station. Opened in 1906, and jointly operated by Great Northern and Northern Pacific Railroads, the station was designed in a grand Italianate style. The modern photograph shows a similar view today with the Alaskan Way Viaduct sweeping past Occidental Park and Occidental Square.

LEFT AND RIGHT: On July 15, 1916, a new company was incorporated in Seattle. At first called Pacific Aero Products Co., it would change its name in 1917 to Boeing Airplane Company and bring the city its greatest spurt in prosperity and growth since the Klondike Gold Rush. So important was the company to Seattle's success that the town became known as Jet City. As the builder of the great bombers of World War II and later pioneer of the civil aviation industry, Boeing ruled the skies for much of the twentieth century. The photograph of the factory floor shows B-17 bombers under construction during WWII, while the second photograph is of Boeing Airfield (now King County International Airport), seen here with Mount Rainier in the background. The airport was dedicated on July 26, 1928.

LEFT AND RIGHT: Ballard's Chittenden Locks (named for the Army engineer General Hiram M. Chittenden) were declared open on July 4, 1917, though the Lake Washington Ship Canal was not officially completed until 1934. The waterway linking Puget Sound to Lake Washington had first been advocated by one of Seattle's first settlers, Thomas Mercer, in 1854. Despite the eighty years that it took to come to fruition, the canal eventually allowed deep draft ships passage into Lake Washington. Lined with public gardens the locks and the canal have since been designated a National Historic District.

Fremont Bridge was built across the Washington Ship canal in 1917. It is a "bascule" bridge, a term Seattleites will be familiar with, meaning that it works like a see-saw in order to allow ships to pass beneath. In the background, and higher than Fremont Bridge, is Aurora Bridge.

LEFT, ABOVE, AND OVERLEAF: Following riots and the exclusion of many of Seattle's Chinese in 1882, the Chinese slowly returned to the city over the following decade, starting another Chinatown on Washington Street before being moved on to King Street as the new Smith Tower increased property values in the area. Later joined by many immigrants from Japan, an Asian community has thrived here ever since, notwithstanding the events of 1942, which saw Japanese citizens forced into internment camps. The photographs opposite and overleaf, both from 1921, show King Street's Chinatown before the area was renamed the International District. The group portrait shows the Lion Dance Group during the Go-Hing Festival. King Street was entered onto the National Register of Historic Places in 1987.

BELOW: Seattle from Queen Anne in 1921. Note the new office buildings to the right of Smith Tower. Though a part of the skyscraper's purpose was to anchor the business district to Pioneer Square, downtown was drifting further north toward Belltown.

RIGHT: The largest office building in the country when it opened in 1924, the Dexter Horton Building on Second Avenue and Cherry was designed by one of the Pacific Northwest's leading architects, John Graham, Sr. A part of the building housed the Dexter Horton National Bank, which later became SeaFirst Bank. The bank was founded by Horton himself, a pioneer who arrived in Seattle in 1853 and was employed at Yesler's mill before buying a store and then moving into banking.

LEFT: The completion of construction on the Olympic Hotel on University Street in 1926 signaled a new benchmark for elegance in the city. Occupying the site of Seattle's original university building, the hotel swiftly became the center of the city's social scene and the hotel of choice for celebrities and the wealthy. Now listed on the National Register of Historic Places, the renamed Fairmont Olympic is still the Pacific Northwest's only AAA standard hotel.

RIGHT: The Kubota Garden in Rainier Beach was the brainchild of Fujitaro Kubota, a self-taught gardener who purchased five acres of swamp in 1927 in order to transform it into a Japanese-inspired garden. Over the years the garden has grown to twenty acres. It is a stunning testament to one man's vision and a beautifully tranquil fusion of Japanese design and the Pacific Northwest landscape.

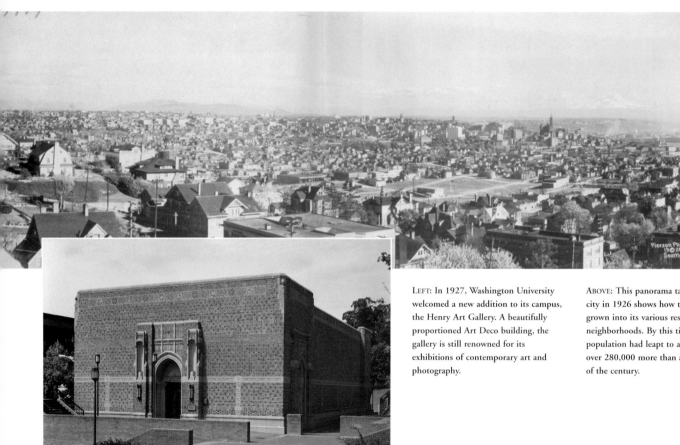

LEFT: In 1927, Washington University welcomed a new addition to its campus, the Henry Art Gallery. A beautifully proportioned Art Deco building, the gallery is still renowned for its exhibitions of contemporary art and photography.

ABOVE: This panorama taken across the city in 1926 shows how the city had grown into its various residential neighborhoods. By this time the city's population had leapt to about 350,000, over 280,000 more than at the beginning of the century.

RIGHT: The story of Seattle's favourite department store, Bon Marché, began in 1890, when Josephine and Edward Nordhoff arrived in the city and opened a small dry goods store. Over the years the Nordhoffs' success saw Bon Marché move to ever-larger Seattle premises (including this one in 1928) and open stores throughout the Northwest. The chain was sold in 2003 to Federated Department Stores, Inc., a year after this photograph was taken, and rebranded Bon-Macy's.

OVERLEAF: The final stage of the Denny Regrade was completed in 1930. This photograph celebrates the occasion and shows the empty lots waiting to be built upon.

WHERE A HILL
WENT DOWN
TO THE SEA:
THE DENNY
REGRADE WORK
COMPLETE

December 28, 1930

A view over greater Seattle in 1928, showing how the downtown area was moving away from the Pioneer Square district close to the base of the Smith Tower at the far right.

LEFT: Dedicated in 1932, the Aurora Bridge (or the George Washington Memorial Bridge as it is properly called) was Seattle's first purpose built highway bridge. Designed by Jacobs & Ober its 2,945-foot span connects Fremont and Queen Anne.

RIGHT: Populated by hundreds of homeless during the Great Depression, Hooverville was a shantytown that sprang up just south of Pioneer Square in the mid-thirties. With the return of prosperity toward the end of the decade many of its poverty stricken citizens found jobs and Hooverville disappeared.

From 1935 to 1967 the extraordinary Art Deco ferry *Kalakala* sailed the waters of Puget Sound. Her futuristic design and sleek lines were unique in ship design and the ferry was fitted to carry 2,000 passengers in style. Sold to an Alaskan fish processor in 1967, *Kalakala* returned to Seattle in 1998. Efforts to restore the ferry are ongoing at the time of going to press.

RIGHT: When it opened on July 2, 1940, the Lake Washington Floating Bridge was the most ambitious floating structure ever designed. Connecting Seattle to Bellevue via Mercer Island, the bridge still serves the city despite modifications and having been sunk during a storm in 1990.

The World Comes to Seattle: 1946-1979

Nighttime on Gayway, Century 21's amusement park area, which boasted rides such as Space Whirl, Trip to Mars, and Meteor.

The World Comes to Seattle: 1946-1979

The postwar period saw Seattle's skyline and world profile steadily rising. While the number of its citizens reached half a million by the mid-fifties, the number of skyscrapers in the new downtown area, north of Pioneer Square, increased. In 1969, Smith Tower was finally relegated to second tallest skyscraper in the city when the SeaFirst Building opened. Civic improvements, such as the creation of the Alaskan Way Viaduct in 1953 and the Evergreen Point Floating Bridge in 1963, renewed the city's infrastructure and catered to the new era of road traffic. In 1962, Seattle also welcomed what would become its most famous landmark. Built for the city's outstanding World's Fair, images of the Space Needle have since graced everything from postcards and t-shirts to the opening credits of *Frasier* ever since. With the war over, Boeing diversified into civil aviation and though the company experienced good times and not quite so good times in the following decades, its continued overall success meant that at the peak of production in the sixties, one in ten Seattleites was employed by Boeing.

1968 saw the approval of $40 million to build more civic amenities, notably the Kingdome, the Aquarium, and Waterfront Park. But while looking to the future, as always, Seattle also began to reassess its heritage. The demolition of the venerable Hotel Seattle on Pioneer Square to make way for an architecturally dissonant parking garage, spurred public debate about conservation, resulting in Pioneer Square being designated Seattle's first protected historic district in 1970. The heart of old Seattle, so long neglected, now saw a steady process of rehabilitation. Conservationists scored another victory in 1971 when Pike Place Market was saved from developers. In 1975, another company that would revolutionize Seattle in a similar way to Boeing, opened its new headquarters in Bellevue. Micro-Soft had arrived.

LEFT AND BELOW: As the importance of road transportation increased during the first half of the twentieth century the railroad tracks that had lined the Seattle waterfront since Victorian times fell out of use. Completed in 1953, the Alaskan Way Viaduct was built on reinforced concrete supports over the old tracks, short sections of which remain in place below.

1962 World's Fair

Seattle's 1962 World's Fair, Century 21, bestowed on the city a lasting legacy. Like the 1909 exposition before, its structures are still in use. The brainchild of one man, Al Rochester, who as a boy had visited the Alaska-Yukon-Pacific Exposition every day it was open, the fair's theme was science and the future, perfect for a decade obsessed with space travel. Century 21 aptly commenced on receiving a radio impulse from a distant star via a telescope in Maine, the radio signal having been initiated by President Kennedy in Florida using the same telegraph equipment as that used by President Taft to open 1909's fair. Including such attractions as Boeing's Spacearium, the Bubbleator (a huge glass globe that visitors could ride through a complex of future worlds), and the Pavilion of Electric Power, the adult-oriented Show Street included a "Girls of the Galaxy" exhibit in which naked women posed for visitors (until the attraction was quickly closed down). Open for only six months, the fair attracted ten million visitors from around the globe including royalty and celebrities (Elvis Presley was a regular while filming *It Happened at the World's Fair*). Century 21 left the city with Seattle Center, worldwide renown, and an enhanced skyline.

LEFT AND FAR LEFT: Construction on the Space Needle commenced just a year before the fair was due to open and finished only just in time. In the week before the opening ceremonies the elevators were still being tested.

ABOVE: Opening day celebrations presided over by the completed 605-foot Space Needle. With a restaurant at 500 feet and an observation deck at 520 feet, the structure was one of the biggest hits of the fair.

ABOVE: The site of Century 21 has been transformed over the subsequent decades into the fabulous Seattle Center, which includes spaces for the performing arts, sports venues, skateboard parks, museums, and fountains.

FAR LEFT: With the site of the World's Fair a mile from downtown, organizers needed to find a way to transport visitors from their hotels. Their appropriately futuristic solution was the Monorail.

LEFT: The fair's elegantly designed futuristic-gothic arches, which still stand today before Seattle Center's Pacific Science Building.

LEFT AND BELOW: The home of the Mariners, the Seahawks, the Sonics, and the Sounders from 1976 to 2000, the Kingdome was Seattle's most controversial building. Despised by many and loved by few, the Kingdome was actually an innovative design and the world's biggest domed stadium at the time of its completion, though even before construction began various pressure groups had been fighting to stop it being built so close to downtown. Nevertheless, it served the city well for twenty-four years before being spectacularly imploded on March 26, 2000.

RIGHT: Since the twenties and thirties downtown had been moving away from the Pioneer Square area, leaving the historic square to sink into decades of neglect until it became the city's first historic district in 1968. While the beautiful Victorian buildings decayed, new concrete skyscrapers were constructed a few blocks north. This photograph shows the Pacific Building, which opened on Third Avenue in 1971.

On the site of the old Kingdome now stands the new Seahawks stadium, Qwest Field. Funded partly by Microsoft's Paul Allen, the new stadium recycled about thirty-five percent of the Kingdome's concrete.

Construction of Waterfront Park, which was to feature Seattle's first proper aquarium began in 1974. The aquarium itself was completed in 1977. Despite financial difficulties that meant drastic cost-cutting it is a superb educational facility and a much-enjoyed landmark.

LEFT: Now ubiquitous around the world, the first ever Starbucks was opened in Pike Place Market in 1971. Named for the first mate in *Moby Dick*, the store sold specialty coffee beans, which quickly found a market in Seattle. By the end of the decade the city had four Starbucks and the company was poised to go global in the eighties.

BELOW: Houseboats have been a common sight on Lake Union since the late nineteenth century when they provided cheap housing for mill workers and fishermen at a time when Seattle's property prices were rising steeply. Later used by students, by the seventies they were becoming more desirable, especially when their numbers were restricted in 1972. Today's houseboats resemble a floating suburb and some are more upscale than the houses on shore.

RIGHT: The Sedgwick James Building on Fourth Avenue is an excellent example of the sleek new skyscrapers, influenced by International Style architects, which were appearing across America in the sixties and seventies. Rising to 344 feet, the pitched roof allows the inhabitants of neighboring towers to keep their views while creating new ones for its own. Completed in 1979, the tower is known locally as the "Darth Vader Building."

The Emerald City: 1980-Today

Seattle in the twenty-first century occupies about 150 square miles, with neighborhoods of many different flavors, from upscale Queen Anne and First Hill to Bohemian Capitol Hill and Fremont, as well as boasting one of the world's premier ports and architecture, museums, galleries, and restaurants to rival any city in the United States. Its rich variety and quality of life still make it one of the most popular places for new settlers, much as it was in the nineteenth century.

The Emerald City: 1980-Today

As the twentieth century drew to a close and the twenty-first began, Seattle witnessed yet another burst of construction work. The eighties alone saw the completion of what are now Seattle's four tallest buildings—Columbia Center, Washington Mutual Tower, Two Union Square, and the Seattle Municipal Tower—along with a host of less dizzying, but architecturally dramatic buildings. A new home was created for the Seattle Art Museum in 1991, while the perennially controversial Kingdome passed into history, to be replaced by Sefeco Field and Qwest Field. Other notable new arrivals included Frank Gehry's amazing Experience Music Project and the Science Fiction Museum in Seattle Center, both funded by Microsoft philanthropist Paul Allen.

As Microsoft came to dominate the growing worldwide computer software industry, many other hi-tech industries opened in and around the city. Although the dotcom bubble burst in the mid-nineties, many internet businesses survive and the city is also of growing importance in the biotech industry as well as still being a booming port city and industrial base. The city's economic success has translated into more wealth and jobs, and a steady rise in newcomers eager for a slice of the good life that Seattle offers—the city now has a metropolitan population approaching 600,000. Wealth has bought with it culture and sophistication. Today's Seattle is richly endowed with orchestras, operas, museums, galleries, cafés, and restaurants, as well as the best shopping in the Pacific Northwest. The city also took center stage globally once more when a new home-grown generation of rockers, led by Nirvana, put "grunge" music at the top of the charts.

Still a relatively young city, Seattle has achieved more than most in a fraction of the time. With the city actively pursuing economic growth and planning ever more ambitious new projects as well as conserving Seattle's unique character and heritage, the future looks bright for the city that was given the official nickname of "Emerald City" in 1985.

RIGHT: Located in the city of Redmond at the eastern edges of Seattle's sprawl, the Microsoft Corporate Headquarters became in the eighties a modern equivalent of Boeing, providing tens of thousands of jobs and attracting other hi-tech industries into the area, particularly during the dotcom boom of the nineties. Founders Bill Gates and Paul Allen have also proven good friends to the city, lavishing tens of millions of dollars on public projects.

OVERLEAF: 1988 saw the opening of the controversial Westlake Center, which had initially been planned twenty years before. Despite the legal wrangling the mall, which is home to over eighty retailers, helped encourage further redevelopment of the surrounding area.

FAR LEFT: Seattle's tallest building since 1985, Columbia Center (seen here to the right of the Municipal Tower) is 882.5 feet from sidewalk to roof.

LEFT: Washington Mutual Tower on Second Avenue is the second tallest skyscraper in the city, measuring 772 feet from base to the tip of its roof pyramid. Opening in 1988, its postmodern design has led to its being nicknamed "the spark-plug" by Seattleites.

RIGHT: One of Seattle's most elegant skyscrapers, the slim silver and white tower of Two Union Square was built in 1989 and is 740 feet tall, or 796.5 feet if the flagpole is included.

LEFT: At 722-foot, Seattle Municipal Tower is the city's fourth highest building. It opened in 1990 as the AT&T Gateway Tower, but was sold to the city in 1996 for $120 million.

RIGHT: Founded in 1933, the Seattle Art Museum was a tenant of a beautiful Art Deco building in Volunteer Park before it moved to this building on University Street in 1991 (the old building now houses the Seattle Asian Art Museum). The "Hammering Man" sculpture in front of the museum, which can also be found in other cities around the world, was added in 1994.

LEFT AND RIGHT: Home of the Seattle Mariners, Safeco Field—seen here in the foreground with Qwest Field behind—held its first ballgame on July 15, 1999. Noted as one of the finest ballparks in the country, Safeco Field allows fans great views of the action wherever their seats. Its retractable roof is an incredible engineering feat, covering nine acres in about ten minutes at the press of a button.

LEFT: Completed in 2000 and located in the heart of the International District to the south of Pioneer Square, the amazing 505 Union Station Building, with its leaning green glass walls, forms part of the Union Station Complex.

RIGHT: Designed by Bassetti Architects and Bohlin Cywinski, and seen here during the last stages of construction, Seattle's newest City Hall was dedicated in 2003. The Municipal Building's replacement is the hub of the Civic Center, providing offices for the mayor, city council, and city attorney.

LEFT: One of Seattle's most recent additions is the Science Fiction Museum, the brainchild of Microsoft founder Paul Allen. Located, appropriately, at the foot of the Space Needle, the museum opened in 2004 with a mission to honor the great Sci-Fi creators and to "invite us to ponder the universe's infinite possibilities."

RIGHT: Paul Allen is also responsible for the Science Fiction Museum's neighbor in Seattle Center, the Frank Gehry-designed Experience Music Project. Dedicated to Seattle native Jimi Hendrix, the project is an outstanding interactive museum devoted to rock n' roll and also features exhibits from legendary Seattle grunge band Nirvana.

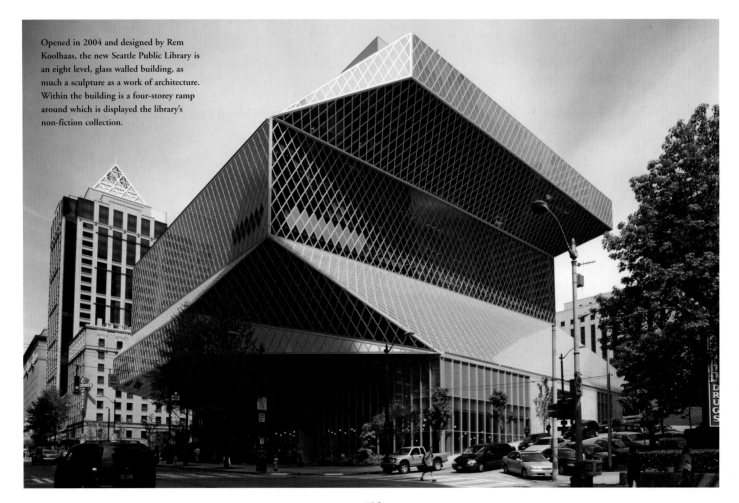

Opened in 2004 and designed by Rem
Koolhaas, the new Seattle Public Library is
an eight level, glass walled building, as
much a sculpture as a work of architecture.
Within the building is a four-storey ramp
around which is displayed the library's
non-fiction collection.

The view over Ballard across Queen Anne and Magnolia to downtown and Greater Duwamish. Seattle's commitment to its parks, begun in 1903 with the commissioning of the Olmsted bothers, has resulted in one of the greenest cities in the nation—despite Seattle's huge urban sprawl—and earned it the official nickname of "Emerald City" in 1985.

Lit up at night, Seattle's skyline fulfils the ambitions of Seattle's original settlers who imagined their city as a rival to New York.